Cat

Written by
Matthew Rayner BVetMed MRCVS

Photographed by
Jane Burton

Gareth Stevens Publishing
A WORLD ALMANAC EDUCATION GROUP COMPANY

Please visit our web site at: www.garethstevens.com
For a free color catalog describing Gareth Stevens
Publishing's list of high-quality books and multi-
media programs, call 1-800-542-2595 (USA)
or 1-800-387-3178 (Canada). Gareth Stevens
Publishing's fax: (414) 332-3567.

Library of Congress Cataloging-in-Publication Data

Rayner, Matthew.
      Cat / written by Matthew Rayner; photographed by
Jane Burton. — North American ed.
      p. cm. — (I am your pet)
      Includes bibliographical references and index.
      Summary: Presents simple information about
cats and choosing one as a pet.
      ISBN 0-8368-4102-6 (lib. bdg.)
      1. Cats—Juvenile literature. [1. Cats. 2. Pets.]
I. Burton, Jane, ill. II. Title.
SF445.7.R38   2004
636.8–dc22   2003066158

This North American edition first published in 2004 by
Gareth Stevens Publishing
A World Almanac Education Group Company
330 West Olive Street, Suite 100
Milwaukee, WI 53212 USA

Original edition copyright © 2004 Bookwork Ltd.,
Unit 17, Piccadilly Mill, Lower Street, Stroud,
Gloucestershire, GL5 2HT, United Kingdom.

Editorial Director: Louise Pritchard
Editor: Annabel Blackledge
Design Director: Jill Plank
Art Editor: Kate Mullins
Gareth Stevens Editor: Jenette Donovan Guntly
Gareth Stevens Designer: Kami M. Koenig

Printed in the United States of America

1 2 3 4 5 6 7 8 9 08 07 06 05 04

Picture credits
t=top b=bottom m=middle l=left r=right
All photographs by Jane Burton except for the following:
Warren Photographic: 4t, 6tr, 6ml, 6bm, 8–9t, 8–9b, 10tl,
10br, 12b, 13tr, 13tm, 16–17b, 17tm, 18l, 20tl, 21t, 22mr,
23l, 26–27b, 28bl, 29ml, 29br

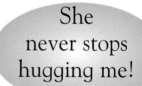

She
never stops
hugging me!

Contents

Words that appear in the glossary are printed in **boldface** type the first time they are used in the text.

Slowly, slowly catchy mousey . . .

The cat's whiskers
My whiskers are important to me.
They are sensitive to touch. I use
them to feel
my way
around.

Who am I?

Feline family

I belong to a large family of animals called **felines**. Wild
felines such as lions, tigers, leopards, and panthers are
some of my cat cousins. I am strong, like them, and can
move easily and quickly. I behave a lot like them, too.

Cat facts

All cats are designed for an active life of hunting. We have good hearing and eyesight. We can run fast, jump, and pounce, too. All cats have large, sharp teeth for eating meat.

Sight and sound
We can see and hear if anything makes even a tiny movement. We also can see in the dark.

All sorts
There are many different kinds of cats. We rarely weigh more than 15 pounds (7 kilograms). We can live for more than twenty years, but most of us live about fourteen years.

Tail talk
We use our tails to help us balance when climbing and running. We also use them to give signals to our friends.

Sharp claws
We keep our claws inside our paws most of the time. This is so they do not get caught when we are moving around. When we need them, we make them spring out.

It takes all sorts

There are lots of kinds of cats, called **breeds**. They come in different colors and with long or short fur. Cats that belong to special breeds are called **pedigreed** cats. Siamese and Burmese are just two kinds of pedigreed cats.

Nonpedigreed cats

All kinds of cats

Where's the hair?

I have some unusual friends, like these two Devon Rex cats. They were bred to have hardly any fur.

All fluffed up

The most common longhaired cat is the **domestic** longhair. In North America, nonpedigreed cats are often called domestic cats.

What a character!

Different breeds of cats have different characters. Most of my friends are very friendly and like to be petted, but others like to be left alone.

Cat coats
Cats have many different
coat colors. Most of
the colors help us
to hide easily when
we are hunting.

I am a
super model.
Why do you think
they call it a
catwalk?

Short story
I am called a
domestic shorthair. I am
not a pedigreed breed, but I am
just as beautiful. My color is silver tabby.

Wild cats

I like living with you in a comfortable home, but I enjoy behaving like my wild relatives, too. Although you feed me, I still like to hunt. If you let me outside, I may fight cats who come too close to my home.

Watch the birdie.

Ears pricked
When I am hunting, I prick up my ears so that I can hear as much as possible.

Creeping cat
This leopard is creeping along very slowly. I can do that, too.

Going

Silent mover
I have pads on the underside of my paws, which help me to move silently. They also protect my feet from rough ground.

wild

My garden
If I am allowed to go outside, I will mark my territory, an area that I think of as mine. I will mark it by rubbing my face on things to leave my scent. This warns other cats to keep away.

Twitchy tail
I may twitch my tail gently to and fro when I am concentrating or excited.

Ready for action
I keep close to the ground when I am creeping up on something. I am then ready to pounce at the right moment.

Wild game
It is fun pretending to hunt. If you pull a toy on a string along the ground, I will creep after it and then pounce.

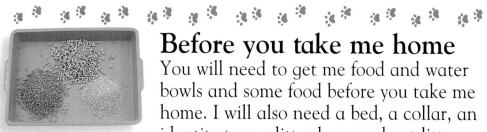

Before you take me home

You will need to get me food and water bowls and some food before you take me home. I will also need a bed, a collar, an identity tag, a litter box, and cat litter.

Litterbug
Give me a litter box so that I can go to the bathroom inside the house.

Catnaps
I will spend a lot of time sleeping around the house and on your lap. I will have a favorite place to sleep where I am not disturbed. This will change from time to time!

Rubber brushes

Metal comb

Stocking up

Pet shops have the best choice of beds, brushes, bowls, food, combs, and collars. Supermarkets may also have the items I need. My **veterinarian**, or vet, may sell cat food and toys for me, too.

Good grooming
I am good at **grooming** myself, but I like being brushed or combed, too. Longhaired cats need grooming every day with a comb to stop knots and tangles from forming.

Metal and bristle brush

Ooooh . . . a
designer label.

Identity tags
If I go outside,
put my address
and telephone
number on my
collar in case I
get lost.

LOOK OUT!
• **Make sure** that my
collar will stretch or
snap easily. Then, if
it gets caught up on
something, it will
not strangle me.

Pick me!

Do you think this is mine?

Where to start
The easiest cats and kittens to find are nonpedigreed. Look for notices of kittens for sale or get a cat from an animal shelter. If you want a pedigreed kitten, you will have to go to a breeder. Try to see the kitten's parents before you choose.

Little cutie
Kittens are cute, but do not forget they soon grow up.

Fit Kitty
A kitten or cat should have a clean nose and eyes and should be alert and playful.

LOOK OUT!
- **Do not** pick a kitten that is very quiet or one with a runny nose or eyes. She may be sick.
- **Take a** new cat or kitten to the vet for a checkup soon after you get her.

Friendly feline
Choose a cat like me, who is friendly and likes to play.

Rescue me!
An animal shelter is a good place to get a kitten or grown-up cat. People at the shelter will make sure she is healthy. You will make a lonely cat happy, too.

Already trained
A grown-up cat like me will be **house trained**. I will ask to go out when I need to.

Feeding time

I must have meat in my diet or I will become very sick. I love cooked chicken and fish, but the easiest and healthiest thing to feed me is ready-made cat food. It comes in different flavors, including chicken and fish!

Mmmm . . . much better than school lunches.

Let's

Eating habits

I like to eat by myself at my own pace. Feed me once or twice a day. Check the package or can to see how much I need.

eat!

LOOK OUT!
- **Do not give** me too much milk. I love milk as a treat, but too much will make my tummy hurt.
- **Do not give** me dog food. It does not contain all the things I need to eat.

Finicky Feline
I can be a fussy eater and will try to make you feed me what I like best. Give me mainly regular cat food or I will get used to eating treats, which may make me fat.

Drink up
Make sure I always have fresh water to drink, especially if I eat dry food. Some of us do not like tap water. If let outside, we will drink rainwater from puddles instead.

Which foods?
Cat food can be canned or dry. I may prefer either dry food or canned food. Dry food is better for my teeth. Canned food contains lots of water. You should feed me canned food if I never go outside. I like a tasty treat sometimes, too.

Canned food

Dry food

Cat treats

Understanding me

Cats talk to each other using different parts of their bodies. I will talk to you this way, too. When you get to know me well, you will understand my **body language**. You will know when I am happy and want to play, when I want to be left alone, and when I am scared or angry.

Cat chat

Happy cat
You will know I am pleased to see you if I rub along your legs. I am leaving my scent on you to mark you as mine!

Purring pussycat
I was able to **purr** when I was only three days old! When I purr, it usually means I am happy and contented, but I may also purr if I am injured and in pain.

Just relax
When a cat is relaxed and playful, he may bat at toys and pounce on them. If he rolls on his back, he may want you to tickle his tummy!

LOOK OUT!
- **Do not** yell at me if I start going to the bathroom outside my litter box. I may be sick or other cats may be picking on me.

All worked up
If a cat is scared or angry, he will stand on his tiptoes and make his fur stand on end. This makes him look bigger. He may wave his tail and hiss at you to warn you away.

Now, if you'd just tickle my tummy . . .

Making friends

When a kitten first comes home, she may be a bit nervous. Let her decide when she wants to get to know you. Do not rush her. She will soon let you handle her and stroke her.

Multi-toes
Some kittens have more than five toes on each paw. This is not usually a problem. Even unusual-looking kittens make very good friends.

Little wriggler
Pick up a kitten under her bottom and chest. Hold her carefully so you do not drop her.

Your

Times two
Two kittens or cats are twice the fun but are also double the trouble!

Playmates
Kittens that live together will spend lots of time playing with each other. They will still want to play with you, too!

Now that will show you who's boss!

It's a habit
I will soon get used to a routine. I will know when to expect you home from school and when I have my meals. I will prefer it if my routine stays the same.

Fierce cats
Most of my friends will not bite or scratch you unless they are very scared or angry. If your cat often attacks you for no reason, ask your vet for advice.

feline friend

Behaving badly
Do not yell at me if I do something wrong. I need you to teach me what is right and wrong. It is always better to reward me when I have been good than to yell at me when I have been bad. Never hit me — you will just scare me.

Swipe it
It is fun to swipe at toys and grab them with my claws.

Frisky feline
I often play games because it is good practice for hunting! I will play with lots of different toys. I like toys that look like small animals, toys that make a noise, and toys that smell like an herb called catnip.

Playtime

Happy cat
Playing makes me feel happy and relaxed.

Mmmm . . . this mouse is a bit chewy!

Sweet smell
I like chewing and rolling on toys that are scented with catnip. The smell makes me feel as playful as a kitten.

Killer instinct
When I pounce on toys and bite them, I am pretending to hunt.

Life's a game
You do not need to buy me expensive toys. I will play with almost anything. I even like playing by myself.

I never grow up

When I am young, I will play all the time. As I grow older, I will not play so much, but there will still be times when I want to play games, so do not throw away my toys.

LOOK OUT!
- **Never let** me play with very fine string or with a needle and thread. I could swallow them, which would be very dangerous.
- **Do not let** me climb the curtains, eat plants, or scratch the furniture. If I get into the habit of doing it, you may not be able to stop me.

Young at heart
In the wild, only kittens play. Adult cats are much too busy hunting. I am still playful, even though I am grown up, because I do not have to worry about feeding myself.

The great outdoors

I love going outside. I go out mainly to hunt and to meet other cats. For safety, you may want to keep me inside all of the time, especially if we live near a road. I can be very happy inside, too.

In and out

Phew! It's good to be home again.

Coming and going
We like the freedom to come and go as we please!

In a flap

The best way to let us in and out is to put a cat flap in your door. We will learn to use it very quickly. Just put some food on the other side and we will soon be running through. You also can get flaps that stop the wrong cats from coming in.

A cat's night out

Some cats, especially male cats, like to wander. If I do not come home one night, I am probably asleep in a shed, garage, or even at the neighbors' house!

Glow-in-the-dark collar

Night prowler

If I go outside at night, give me a glow-in-the-dark collar so drivers can see me.

Dangerous world

Going outside can be fun, but it can also be dangerous. The biggest danger is traffic. Try to keep me away from roads or consider keeping me inside.

Ear, ear
Check my ears for wax buildup.
If I have itchy ears, I may
have mites.

Healthy

Checking up
Check me over every
day. You can do this
when I am sitting on
your lap. Take me
straight to the
vet if you are
worried.

Clean cat
If I stop
grooming
myself, I
may be
sick.

Poor paw
Check my
paws for
cuts and
swelling.

cat

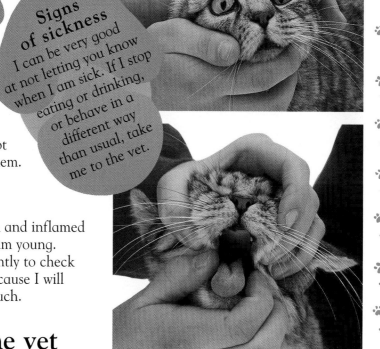

Signs of sickness
I can be very good at not letting you know when I am sick. If I stop eating or drinking, or behave in a different way than usual, take me to the vet.

Bright eyes
Check my eyes to make sure that they are not runny or red and to make sure that they do not have anything in them.

Open wide
I can get dirty teeth and inflamed gums even when I am young. Open my mouth gently to check them. Be careful because I will not like this very much.

Visiting the vet
Take me to the vet once a year for a checkup and for **vaccinations**. I need flea and **worming** treatments, too. You can buy these from the vet. If I make it difficult for you to treat me, ask the vet to do it.

Tail trouble
If my tail is bent or crooked, take me to the vet, because it may be broken.

Feel the fur
Check my skin for injuries and for fleas. Use a flea spray to kill the fleas, but I probably will not like it!

Free spirit

I am an independent animal, which means I like to do what I want when I want. I need time on my own, but I like company and affection, too. I especially enjoy being petted by you.

Warm welcome
I will not be lonely when you are at school, but I will be happy to see you when you get home. I will trot up to you and rub my scent on your legs — be careful not to trip over me!

You and me
Once I trust you, I will grow to love you.

Cat company

Oooh, please just leave me alone!

Who are you?

Cat meets cat
When two kittens meet for the first time, there should not be a problem. If you already have a cat in your home, introduce a new kitten to her very slowly.

Circling around
When kittens first meet, they may circle around to check each other out.

Friend or foe?
We will live happily with other cats and dogs, but do not let us meet rabbits, rats, mice, parakeets, or guinea pigs, because we will think they are food. Keep us apart at all times.

LOOK OUT!
• **Never leave** me to look after myself. If you go on vacation, ask a friend to take care of me. You could take me to a **boarding kennel**, but only if I have had my vaccinations. If I have not, I may get sick from another cat.

Mom-to-be

When a female cat gives birth, it is known as kittening. Cats usually have kittens in the spring and summer. Females can have up to eight kittens. Together, they are called a litter.

Tiring work
A mother cat needs lots of peace and quiet. Being a mom is hard work.

Having kittens

Watch those sharp claws!

Feeding the young
Kittens drink milk from their mother. She needs to eat about three times more than usual to make enough milk for them all.

Newborn
Kittens are born deaf and blind. Their mother looks after them carefully.

Where do you think you are going?

Growing up
Kittens can see and hear at three weeks old and will start to explore. Their mother will not let them go far. She will bring them back in her mouth.

Off we go
Kittens can leave home at ten weeks old. By then, they do not need their mother's milk anymore and she has taught them all she can.

Glossary

boarding kennel
A boarding kennel is a place where your cat can stay for a short time. She will be well fed and cared for.

body language
Cats use their bodies to show other cats and people what they are thinking and feeling. This is called body language.

breeds
Breeds are special types of cats. Siamese cats are one breed of cat.

domestic
In North America, a domestic cat means a mixed-breed cat. The term can also mean cats that have been bred to live in the company of humans.

felines
Cats belong to a family of animals called felines. Lions and tigers are felines, too.

grooming
When you brush a cat's fur, it is called grooming. Cats also groom themselves with their tongues.

house trained
A kitten needs to be taught to go to the bathroom outside or to use a litter box inside. This is called being house trained.

pedigreed
A pedigreed cat has a family that includes only animals of the same breed, such as all Siamese cats.

purr
When kittens and cats are happy, they purr, or make a soft growling noise like a motor.

vaccinations
Cats need to have vaccinations, usually by getting shots, to stop them from catching diseases.

veterinarian
A short term for veterinarian is vet. A vet is a doctor for animals. You should take your cat to the vet if she is sick or injured and to give her vaccinations.

worming
A cat can get worms inside her. These may make her sick. A vet will help you get rid of the worms.

Find out more . . .

Web Sites

**www.americanhumane.org/
kids/cats.htm**
This web site created by
the American Humane
Society gives all sorts of
tips from choosing a cat
breed to growing a yummy
garden for your new kitty.

www.animaland.org
This fun web site for the
American Society for the
Prevention of Cruelty to
Animals (ASPCA) has
games, cartoons, a
pet care guide, and
much more!

**www.feline-
behavior.com**
This web site offers
information about
behavior problems,
body language,
training, and
cats in the wild.

Books

*Calico's Cousins: Cats from
Around the World.*
Phyllis Limbacher Tildes
(Charlesbridge Publishing)

How to Talk to Your Cat.
Jean Craighead George.
(HarperCollins)

You should
read this — there's
some interesting
stuff here!

Index